Christy's Book

by Mary Burch

Dedicated to my precious daughters,

**Debbie, Carol, Diane,
Starla & Christy**

Christy's Book

Published by AuthorHouse 01/28/2015

ISBN: 978-1-4969-6439-7 (sc)
ISBN: 978-1-4969-6440-3 (e)

Library of Congress Control Number: 2015900746

Any people depicted in stock imagery provided by Thinkstock are models,
and such images are being used for illustrative purposes only.
Certain stock imagery © Thinkstock.

This book is printed on acid-free paper.

All Photographic Images Property of Mary Burch
Hearts Designed by Christy Burch
Interior and Cover Designer Carolyn Bernal
Vector Images licensed to Carolyn Bernal

AuthorHouse™
1663 Liberty Drive
Bloomington, IN 47403
www.authorhouse.com
Phone: 1 (800) 839-8640

authorHOUSE®

Author's Note

*T*his book I'm now writing is for my 40 year old handicapped daughter, Christy. She sees me at the computer all the time writing, and one day, asked me,

   "Mom, my book"

She meant to say, I want to write a book about my life. After much thought about how to put into words her life as she remembers it, here is her book. So, I hope you will learn and love reading about Christy's life.

When I was pregnant with Christy, I felt that something was different than when I had my other children. She didn't move inside my tummy like the other babies did. Christy is the youngest of four daughters. She sustained permanent brain damage during the early stages of my pregnancy.

Mary Burch

I took her to a well-known university hospital when she was just four years old, and after four days of being tested by the doctors, they came into my room and told me,

"We are so sorry to have to tell you this and we would like to tell you first that you have done a wonderful job in caring for your daughter. Mrs. Burch, your little Christy, will never reach beyond the age between a seven to nine-year-old child."

The doctors didn't know what could have caused it. Until a few years later they discovered that the morning sickness pill prescribed was causing birth defects such as brain damage, and also deformities. When I was pregnant with her, I took the pills for morning sickness.

We contacted an attorney that already had around 600 clients that he was representing and planning a lawsuit against the makers of a medication prescribed for nausea and vomiting of pregnancy.

At first I was extremely concerned at the thought of having a special needs child, but as the years passed I began to realize what a special child she would become. Not only to me, but to everyone who would come to know her.

It had been ten years since my last child was born, and the Doctors told me I could never have another baby because of a very serious female problem I had endured years earlier. So low and behold one day I found out I was expecting again, I was elated, and more than ready for another baby. I had dreamed of having at least ten children and live in a big two story house. I never got my two story house, but I did get five beautiful little girls.

Now here is Christy's story.

Mary Burch

Chapter

Coming from a very backward and uneducated family right out of the backwoods of Arkansas, I had never been exposed to someone who had a mental disability. We came to California when I was just a young girl of nine. We had never been exposed to much of the outside world, so when we saw someone who acted differently from us, we were told they were crazy and to stay clear of them. Back in the fifties when I was just a young girl, we had never heard of,

Anxiety, Obsessive Compulsive Disorder,
Bipolar Disorder, Eating Disorder,
Depression, Suicide,
Attention Deficit Hyperactivity Disorder,
Schizophrenia, Autism.

Those kind of people were never talked about very much. When they were mentioned, it was kept very hush, hush. About all we heard about was that they had to be taken to the insane asylum, where they were kept under lock and key twenty-four hours a day. I remember my poor old grandpa, when he came to live with us; he was in his eighties and couldn't remember a thing past my father's tenth birthday. We would tease him, and he would chase us all over the house trying to hit us over the head with his walking cane. We were told that he had the old-timers' disease, so he didn't need to be locked up cause everyone got it when they reached a certain age. I remember one time someone from the church had to be locked up cause he was acting crazy. My father thought he could heal him. So, we all got into the old car, and daddy drove us down to the crazy place way across town. He took all five of us kids in and we went all through

Grandparents Burch

Mary Burch

the place, he wanted us to see him pray for the man and watch him be healed. He thought it would be a good lesson for us kids.

I was never so scared in my life. There were crazy people all over the place. They couldn't reach us as though to hurt us cause they were behind locked doors. We could see them through the windows; some were rocking back and forth, some were talking out loud to someone, but no one was there. Some were sitting and crying calling out for help, just staring at us; I will never forget that day as long as I live. Well, daddy prayed for the man, but he never got any better. I couldn't wait to get out of there and go home. Then one day it happened in our family, my youngest sister had just had a baby girl, and when the baby was just a few months old, my sister had a stroke. She would just sit and stare at us not able to say a word for about a month, and

Grandma and my Mom

Mary Burch

then slowly she began to communicate with us again. My sister would never be the same; she would have to be taken care of for the rest of her life, which, of course, became my mother's job. By that time we all had married and left home, so she had Jena all to herself, her and her baby girl. We all had been told about and had seen people who had been a victim of a stroke, but we didn't know about anyone being born with a mental illness, until Christy's birth.

My labor pains started early in the morning on May 15, 1974, just before the other girls were up and got ready for school. I tried not to wake them, but all of a sudden my water broke, and we had to get them up and prepared for their little brother or sister. We didn't want to know the sex of the baby before it was born. We all wanted to be surprised. Her sisters were so excited they couldn't wait to hold her, and love her. They were just beside themselves when I went in and got them out of bed that morning and told them that this is the day. You're all going to have to share mom with a little brother or sister. They were running around the house bumping into one another not knowing what to do first. They all wanted to come to the hospital with us, but I told them no because I didn't know how long it would be before the baby was born. We promised to call the school as soon as the baby made its appearance. My oldest daughter was fifteen, my third daughter was two years younger than the oldest, and my fourth daughter would be ten years older than the baby.

I was dreading going through childbirth again; this would be my fifth child, and I knew what to expect. My first one took three days to make her appearance, my second one took about three or four hours; my third one took two days, and Starla took twelve hours. The drive to the hospital seemed to take forever. My husband got me checked in and took care of the paperwork. Then he decided that he would have enough time to go over to his mom and dad's for a cup of coffee. I didn't want him in the labor room with me. I wanted to be alone so that I could suffer in my own way without having to worry about making him or anyone else feel sorry for me. As my mom found out, she came running into the labor room crying. I begged her just to go home that we would call her when it was over. Oh no, she couldn't do that she said, she wanted to stay with me until the baby was born. Well, thanks for my big brother coming in and almost having to carry her out of the room crying. I looked over at him as he was ushering her out the door and mouthed the words thank you.

My Dad

Mary Burch

My beautiful little Christy came into the world before her dad had time to make it to his parent's house for coffee. It was 10:01 A.M. The girls had just gotten into their class when they got the call. The birth was very easy. It went well with no problems at all. Except that she had dark hair all over her body, I had never seen a baby like that I was terrified that something was wrong. The doctor just laughed at me and said,

"Not to worry, in few days all of it will fall off." Which, of course it did. All of the nurses and doctors said that she was one of the most beautiful babies they had ever seen. There was always a group of people just standing at the nursery window staring at her. I was elated. I hadn't been able to enjoy

Baby Christy

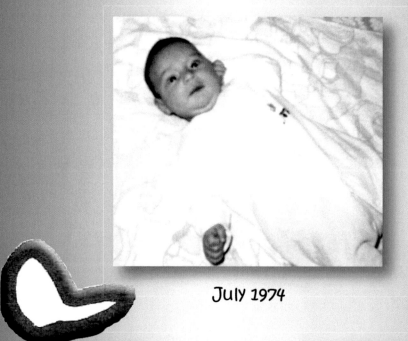

July 1974

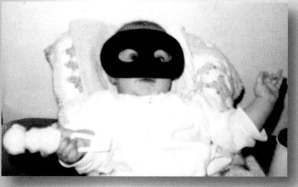

October 1974

Mary Burch

my other babies in a way that I needed to; I was so young when I had them. I was only 15 years old when I had my first one. Being so young and having to work and also not having a good and stable marriage, my little babies didn't have the completely devoted mom they deserved. Of course, I loved all of my babies the same. But being older now, and able to be a stay at home mom and having the help of my other girls, I was looking forward to this one so much.

Her sisters were so much help; I don't know what I would have done without them. Her first few months at home with us were filled with her crying almost day and night. Finally, the Doctor gave me some medicine for colic and the crying stopped. One day when we were lying on the bed I held up a little toy and started making it swing back and forth in front of her eyes. She wasn't following its

 I was born here.

movements. She was just staring straight ahead. My heart started pounding in my chest, I could tell by the blank stare that something was wrong with her. She was so beautiful and healthy I couldn't believe what I saw, she showed no signs of any kind of disability. I didn't say anything to the girls or her dad, I pretended like everything was all right. I didn't want to believe that anything could possibly be wrong with her.

She didn't start walking until she was fifteen months old, and had a very hard time with her balance. I noticed she had a slightly forward slope. She wasn't talking like the other girls did when they were her age. One day when she was about two years old. I was holding her in my arms out in the front yard when a plane was flying over. I pointed towards the sky and said,

"Look a plane! Say plane, Christy."

Sisters

Mary Burch

I tried to get her to say the word plane, but she just looked at me, and didn't respond. Then, there was that time when she was about three years old. Her dad and I had been arguing that day. We were standing in the hallway, and Christy came up to us, and she took her dad's hand and then mine and made us hold hands. I couldn't believe what she just did. I knew then that even though she had a problem she was in some ways very intelligent. I don't think that anyone has ever been loved more than Christy. Her sisters were crazy about her. They carried her around all of the time, loving her, playing with her, feeding her and babysitting her when I had to be somewhere.

One day we were planning on going to the store. I was taking too long to get ready to go, and she got tired of waiting on me. So she walked up to me and just as clear as could be said, "Go to store now mom",

Christy

1976

1977

Mary Burch

and stomped her feet. I had never heard her ever speak a word before; I nearly fainted.

When she was four years old, I decided to enroll her into preschool. I'll never forget her very first day there. I was standing and talking to her teacher when she said to me,

"Look over there",

and she pointed at Christy. She was sitting at the table with her head down and her lips turned down like she was about to cry, our first day apart, I did cry. I stayed with her as long as I could, but I could tell the teacher wanted me to leave, so she could get into and meet all of her students and get the class in order. So, I went home and cried my eyes out, I didn't know if I would be able to let her go or not.

She finally got used to going to school and began to

First Day of PreSchool
1977

Mary Burch

like it very much. I was there most of the time with her, helping the teachers as much as I could while trying to stay out of their way. She met her first puppy love at preschool, "Albert" he was a little blond haired blue eyed cutie, and just as sweet as he was cute. When we would take the children on an outing for the day, they would always be together. They would hold hands and walk as close to one another as they could get. They were just five years old it was beautiful. We always planned fun things for the children. One time, we all went to a dairy so they could learn where their milk came from. After the tour, we all sat down on the owner's front lawn, and they served us ice cream in the little paper cups that use to be so popular. When the school year ended, we had a graduation at the Ceres Park in a beautiful little rose garden. She still remembers that day as if it was yesterday. Right after the graduation was over, her teacher pulled me aside and told me she had something she wanted to talk to me about. I was thinking it was about her going into first grade the next year, but what she said to me that day will live with me forever.

"Mrs. Burch, I'm sorry to have to tell you this, but I don't think Christy will be able to attend regular school. From my experience, I can see that she has a serious learning disability."

She didn't have to tell me anymore, I already knew that, I was just hoping that she would outgrow it and be able to go to school like the rest of the students.

When we got home, I called her doctor, and told him what her teacher had said.

"Well, he told me, even if there is something wrong with her, there's nothing we can do about it anyway."

Mary Burch

DEC 82

Mom and sisters

Mary Burch

I was livid, and that was the last time I ever had any contact with him. I called around and found another doctor. When we took her in for her first visit with him, he told us to take her to Stanford University. He said that they had the best specialist in our area. So off we went to Palo Alto. We spent four days there, and Christy saw the best doctors available. After they had finished their evaluation, they all came to the same conclusion. Christy would never progress any further than a seven to nine-year-old child mentally. Physically she looked very healthy, just passing her in the street you would never guess that anything was wrong with her.

The following year I enrolled her into the Center for the Developmentally Disabled and Handicaped, she seemed just to fall into place there, and all of her teachers just fell in love with her. She would come

Grandparents Rost

Mary Burch

home in the afternoon with hearts, butterflies, and smiles painted on her arms with water color paint. She told me that a teacher named 'John Wray' did it. Over the years, John would become like family to Christy; she grew to love him as did all of his students. He would become one of the most important figures in most all their lives. I remember one time we had gone to the grocery store, all at once she pulled away from me, and started running toward a man and woman. She ran into the man's arms, and he picked her up and gave her a hug. As I got closer, I heard the woman say,

"So, you're the other women."

Christy was repeating over and over John's name. She still loves him just as much to this day. John would become her teacher as she moved on up to another class when she was older, as I recall she was around fifteen years old. It was during that time that she had her three-year update 'Psychologist

Mary Burch

Report'. In observing Christy, it is noted that she is an energetic girl with an interest in things in her immediate environment. She asks a lot of questions with a combination of sign language, verbal expressions, and gestures to communicate with others. Her verbal responses consist of only one or two words at a time.

Christy was cooperative during the assessment and responded to the tasks presented. It was apparent that some of her responses were just given without checking for the appropriateness at the time, however. Scores on the Stanford-Binet indicate a mental age of five years and a score of 36. She was successfully able to pass all items at the four-year level with sporadic successes noted in the next three levels. Strengths were noted in vocabulary. Week areas indicate the ability to discriminate between pictures, which depict similarities and differences.

Christy's Family

Mary Burch

Both fine and gross motor skills show significant delays. Her attempts to copy a "square" and a "rectangle" resulted in circles mostly. She was unable to follow a path with her pencil without errors. She knows her primary colors, but experiences difficulty with number concepts using "blocks" as objects.

Christy attempted drawings of her family; these depicted only "heads" with facial features included but not bodies.

Summary/Recommendations

Christy is still functioning within the "SH level". Her communication skills are severely limited, although she utilizes several modes of communication. She was given "A Vineland Adaptive Behavior Scale" and her scores indicate about an average age of four years.

Christy

Mary Burch

Continued placement in Christy's present program is recommended.

"Christy would spend the rest of her life in programs for the developmentally disabled."

While still at a center for the developmentally disabled, Christy would fall in love with "Bill", her second love. John would hold dances for the students on special holidays. Some of the students could really get out there, and "cut a rug", so to speak. Christy loved going to the dances and socializing with all of her friends. Bill was attending a training center located right next door to the center for the developmental disabled where Christy was attending. He would always show up at the dances and would always ask her to dance. Well, she just fell head over heels in love with him. Until one night while they were holding each other close and dancing a slow dance he just all of a sudden pulled away from her and left her standing there. He went over

Bill

Mary Burch

to another girl and asked her to dance. Well, Christy didn't know what to do. So I went and got her off of the floor and sat with her while she was just staring at Bill and the other girl dancing together. I could see the hurt in her eyes. I felt like crying for her but tried to make light of it. She never would forget her first or second love. She still talks about both of them today, and about how Bill left her standing on the dance floor all alone. Bill would eventually marry the other girl. They had lived at the same group home together for many years. The owner of the home would oversee the wedding and their lives together. Tragically, his wife would pass away not too long after their marriage. Christy and Bill still see each other at the dances that John holds for all of them but it's not the same now between them. Like the old saying go's, "when its over, its over", even for the developmentally disabled.

Mary Burch

3
Chapter

Christy was 16 years old when she had her first seizure. She was at the Flea Market with her sister Starla and her dad. They were selling a few items and took her with them, for her outing for the day. Christy had a habit of putting her right hand up over her eyes and moving it back and forth in the sun, the Doctor said it was one of her ways of entertaining herself. It would take her into a mild hypnotic state. Only this time it took her farther than that. All of a sudden she fell to the ground, she was having a seizure. She had never had one before, and her dad and sister didn't know what was happening to her. They called an ambulance and got her to the hospital. Both of them were scared to death, not knowing what was going on.

Christy and her dad

Mary Burch

Neither one of them had ever seen anyone have a seizure before. I had been out of town visiting relatives, when I got the call I thought I would have a wreck in my car before I made it home. I was devastated, now I had something new to worry about. Her Doctor put her on a medication for seizures right away. I took her home, and she was fine for about three weeks. Then one day when we were having lunch at her favorite place to eat she started to shiver, I felt her forehead and she had a mild fever. I thought maybe she was getting a cold. I took her home and cared for her for a couple of days. She wasn't getting any better, so I took her to her Doctor, and he told me to take her to the hospital. As she continued to get worse, I stayed for several days in the room with her day and night. Her lips started cracking and bleeding, and she couldn't even get up and walk to the bathroom, we had to use a bedpan. I was terrified! Then one day

Mom and Dad

Mary Burch

a nurses aid came walking into her room, she looked over at Christy and said,

"Oh I see she has an allergic reaction to the seizure medication."

I was stunned,

"What makes you think that?" I asked her.

"Because my husband had the same symptoms when he found out he was allergic to it."

I called the nurse in right away, and told her what she had said. I then told her to not ever give her anymore of that seizure medication. She told me,

"well she would have another seizure if we don't, and you will be responsible."

"I'll take that chance, I said. Just don't give her that medication."

I called her Doctor and told him what was going on. He had been treating her for flu symptoms. He knew that she was taking a new medication for seizures and didn't even stop to think that she may be

Mary Burch

having an allergic reaction to it.

Well, as soon as I got her home from the hospital I called and made an appointment with a neurologist. They ran some tests and found that she had been having Petit Mal seizures and Grand Mal at the same time. She had been having the Petit Mal all of her life and no one could even tell she was in one.

Her new Doctor put her on two different types of medications. So I have to be very careful and not let her be in the sun too long, so far she has only had a couple of mild ones over the years. The medication is working very well this time.

After graduating from the Center for Developmentally Disabled, Christy went on to another program called Citywise she loved the new program and one of her teachers from the Center was the Program Director, so she felt right at home there. All of her favorite friends went there also. It was held in another town just a few miles away, so she really felt like she was growing up now. They had a work program outside of the classroom that the students could go and be involved in the community. She would come home with all kinds of stories to tell every day. One of the jobs that she was on was working in a nursing home. The students went there to visit the elderly and sick, one of her favorite people was an older gentlemen. His name was Joe, I think she favored him because she had an uncle named Joe. When old Joe, as she called him, passed away she was heart broken. She came home telling me about it and started crying, and so did I. Another job that they had the students doing was cleaning the bathrooms for a pizza place. I put a stop to that as soon as I found out. I didn't want

Christy 🤍

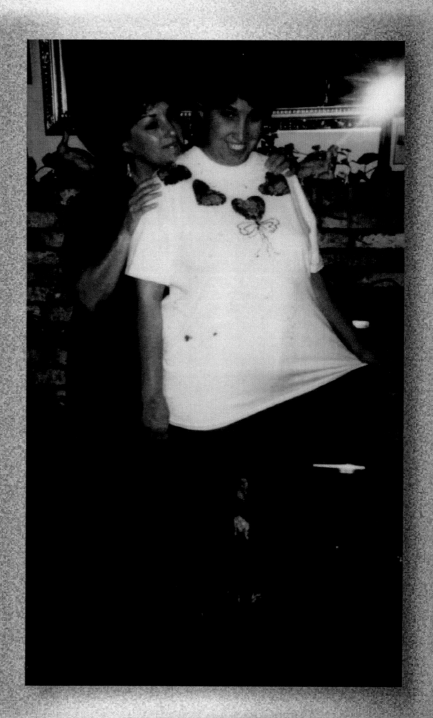

Mary Burch

her cleaning up after the general public after they just got through using the restroom. That was the only time I had any concern about what kind of job they had the students doing. Most of the students were not capable of understanding about their own hygiene much less anyone else's. Another job the students did was to work at a clothing store, stacking boxes.

When she was ready to graduate from Citywise they held a big ceremony for the students, they filmed it, and she had her teacher help her write a speech, she looked so beautiful. That is the picture she chose for the front cover for her book. My beautiful little Christy was growing up. She was twenty-two years old now and still at the seven to nine-year level. At this time, we decided that she would go on to a place called Community Continuum College. She loved this program also, a lot of her best friends moved on to this program along with her. When I found out they had a little beauty shop for the students, I right away put in my application to work there. I had been a cosmetologist for many years and always kept my license current. After a few months their hairdresser had to leave, so I got a call one day to come to work, I was elated. I would only work one day a week, but that was fine with me. I just wanted to be close to Christy and all of her lifelong friends.

I would spend the next ten years cutting and styling their hair and getting more hugs and kisses and love that anyone could ever imagine. It seems so strange that when I am with my students they seem normal to me, I don't even think of them having any developmental disability at all. I've said many times over the years that I wished all of my kids were just like Christy. She has given me unconditional love

Christy's Book

for thirty-nine years, and I'm praying that I have that many more years with her. Over the years, she has become my caregiver. If I am tired and sitting in my favorite chair, she will go into the bathroom and get a warm washcloth and then will sit down on the footstool and wash my feet. Then she will put lotion on them, the whole time not saying a word. And when I am sitting in my chair having a late lunch or dinner, I can see her out of the corner of my eye watching me. As soon as I take my last bite she jumps up and carries my tray into the kitchen for me. I have never asked her to do any of these things. If she sees someone that needs help with anything, she will jump up without being asked and just go do it. We were at the store the other day, and there was an older couple walking in just ahead of us. Christy started walking faster; she went around them and pulled out a cart and gave it to them. They just stood looking at her for a

Mary Burch

moment, then they said well thank you so much, it's not everyday that someone does that for us. Christy said, "welcome." She still at this time in her life can only speak in two to three word sentences. She is so loving and trustful of everyone that she can never go outside alone. She has to have someone with her every hour of the day and night, especially at meal time. Part of her throat and tongue was paralyzed when she sustained the brain damage. All of her food whether it be meat or vegetables have to be cut into bite size pieces. If she is not careful, her food will just slide down her throat without her feeling it, and she will choke. She almost choked to death on a grape one time. It takes four hundred movements of the tongue just to make one syllable. That is the reason she has a speech impediment.

Her uncle Jess owned a horse that we kept on our little acre for him. She loved her uncle so much

Mary Burch

Christy

and

Mom

Christy's 39th Birthday

that every time he would come to feed the horse; she would insist that I make him coffee or a sandwich that she could take out to him. Her greatest pleasure in life is doing things for other people. Her teachers at the college told me that she is always helping the other students who are not as able to get around as she is. She is always coming up behind a teacher and rubbing their back, and giving them a back message. Her uncle Jess made a comment one day that the world would be so much better off if everyone were just like Christy. One morning he came a little early and when she ran out to greet him, he acted like he was scared of her. She looked at him as if to say, whats wrong uncle Jess? He told her, you just scared me to death, you don't have your makeup on, she came in the house as fast as she could and went in and put on some makeup. She could do a pretty good job all by herself; one of the classes in her program had a makeup class,

Love –
N grace

Nancy Grace

Mary Burch

and she always wanted to be in that class. She had a wonderful teacher named Commie. She was very loving and had a lot of patience with the students. Her program at CCC was like a school setting, all of the students changed rooms every hour so that they wouldn't get too bored. After I had left as their hairdresser, I became a member of the 'Board of Directors' for the next four years. I always tried to be involved as much as possible in her activities. At their yearly prom dance at CCC a few months ago, she had her picture taken and she looked so beautiful.

I have worked with the developmentally disabled for over thirty years; they are all so different, there are thousands of levels of disabilities. They have taught me so much, and given me so much love that I can't imagine my world without them. The teacher that I talk about in the book, John Wray

John Wray

is not just a retired teacher, he is to some of these special people, their world. He is the one who holds the 'Special Olympics' every year and has done so for many, many years, along with the dances. And I know he will continue to do so until the day comes which I hope, is a long time off, until he just can't do it anymore. John Wray is loved and respected by so many people, all of the students, all of the parents and all who are involved in the activities that he holds for our very, very special people.

"A special thank you John for being who you are and for all of the time and love that you have given to our children."

When Christy was around twenty-five years old, I wrote her a poem.

Mary Burch

John Wray
you are the BEST

Thank You

CHRISTY'S POEM

I'm shuttled here and shuttled there, sometimes
I think they just don't care. I know they do but
in my heart, sometimes I feel so far apart. Apart
from all the special things, the things I know that
life should bring.

Like having babies, driving cars, going places near
and far. I know these things cannot be, for someone has to care for me. Oh, how I long to do just
one, one of these things before they're gone.

I have my place in time you see. I feel the love sur-
rounding me. All my friends they try their best, to
make me happy like the rest.

My mommy tells me all the time that I was sent
through space and time, I was sent from up
above, just to comfort and to love.

Mary Burch

To be with her until the time,
the light in her no longer shines.

A special little book written just for a
special little girl.

Love You Forever,
Mom
2013

Printed in the United States
By Bookmasters